For Mature Audiences

A creampie can be something people want to explore

"Am I too full? Or can I fit in some more?"

A creampie can be warm and make a mess

A creampie can drip onto your dress

Be careful having a creampie outdoors

A creampie can be enjoyed on all fours

Sometimes a creampie can happen accidentally

A creampie can taste heavenly

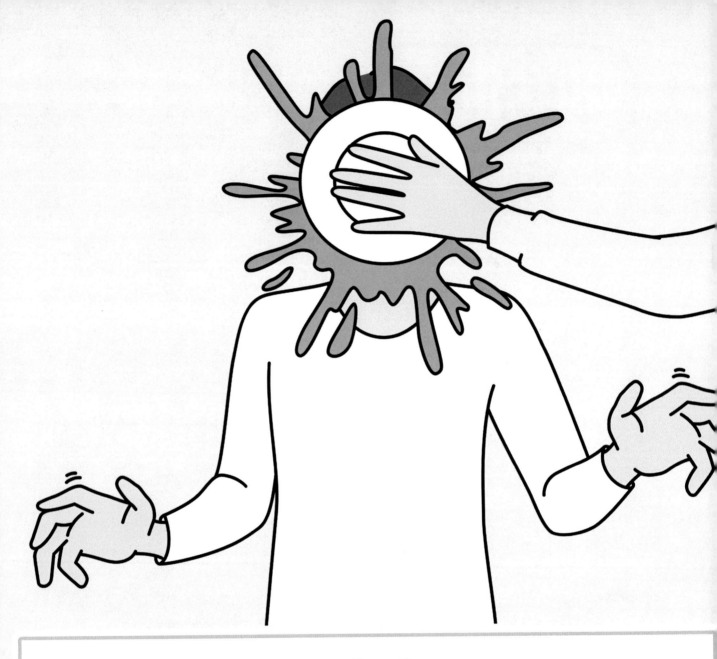

A creampie to the face can come with some force

Sharing a creampie with someone else can cause divorce

⚠ WARNING

CREAM PIES TO THE FACE CAN CAUSE SORE EYES AND BLURRY VISION!

Creampies should come with a warning

Sometimes creampies can make you sick in the mornings

A cream pie can come as quite a surprise

Be careful not to get cream in your eyes

Infected eyes can be sore and hurt

Sometimes creampies can squirt

Creampies can be enjoyed by many

**Molly loves a cream pie
and so does Jenny**

Some may sell cream pies for money

FREE HOMEMADE CREAM PIES!

FREE CREAM PIES

Some people give cream pies away for free

If you're offered a creampie, just take it

About The Author

Jen Jenivive

Loves a cream pie. Fan of silly, immature humour

@jenjenivivereads

Check out my other books on Amazon